PEACE

ON THE
HOME FRONT

**Always find a way to gather with other
believers (Hebrews 10:24-25):**
*And let us consider one another in order to stir up
love and good works, not forsaking the assembling
of ourselves together, as is the manner of some,
but exhorting one another, and so much the more
as you see the Day approaching.*

Published by

WORD PRODUCTIONS

battlefieldprayers.com
wordproductions.org
lifetotheworldministries.org

Always find a way to gather with other believers (Hebrews 10:24-25):

And let us consider one another in order to stir up love and good works, not forsaking the assembling of ourselves together, as is the manner of some, but exhorting one another, and so much the more as you see the Day approaching.

If you have been blessed by this ministry, would you be willing to donate to help get these materials into the hands of those serving our country in the field?

Go to:
www.lifetotheworldministries.org OR
www.battlefieldprayers.com

Contents

❧

Chapter   **Page**

Part One

Prayers & Promises for Peace

CHAPTER ONE

Completely New!

A GOOD START

*Dear Father in heaven,
I consecrate my life to you. Thank You
for sending Jesus Christ to die on the
cross for my sins and rise from the dead
on the third day. I accept Him as my
Savior and Lord. Jesus, come into my
heart by Your Holy Spirit, right now. Be
the Lord and Redeemer of my life. Take
control of my life, fill me with Your
Holy Spirit, and make me holy
according to Your sovereign plan. I ask
You to reveal Yourself to me, and what
it means to me personally. I am trusting
You, the Creator of all things, to lead
me into all truth. I commit my life,
spirit, soul, and body into Your keeping,
in Jesus' name. Amen.*

~Scriptural Confirmation~

For God so loved the world that He gave His only begotten Son, that whoever believes in Him should not perish but have everlasting life. John 3:16

And this is eternal life, that they may know You, the only true God, and Jesus Christ whom You have sent. John 17:3

For unto us a Child is born, unto us a Son is given; and the government will be upon His shoulder. And His name will be called Wonderful, Counselor, Mighty God, Everlasting Father, Prince of Peace. Isaiah 9:6

In whom we have redemption through His blood, the forgiveness of sins, according to the riches of His grace. Ephesians 1:7

When the fullness of the time was come, God sent forth His Son, made of a woman, made under the law, to redeem them that were under the law, that we might receive the adoption of sons. Galatians 4:4, 5

How much more shall the blood of Christ, Who through the eternal Spirit offered Himself without spot to God, purge your conscience from dead works to serve the living God? And for this cause He is the Mediator of the new testament, that by means of death, for the redemption of the transgressions that were under the first testament, they which are called might receive the promise of eternal inheritance. Hebrews 9:14, 15

Christ our passover is sacrificed for us. 1 Corinthians 5:7

First Things First

There is a good reason why the prayer to accept Christ Jesus as your personal Lord and Savior is at the front of this book.

Even if you aren't sure it is real or works, I counsel you to try it, bearing in mind that the prayer even requests God to show you if it is real. Pray with an open heart, truly asking God Himself to show you if Jesus is real and what this means to you. I guarantee you that it will work because He is a living, vital, and real God. When I prayed that prayer very skeptically years ago, I felt love on the inside of me for the first time in my life.

I didn't want man's opinion...I grew up with that. I had to know for myself that He was real.

Any successful program for change that you have read about includes the spiritual aspect. You are not just a body. You have a spiritual person on the inside of you who needs a real "touch" by the living God, who is Spirit. There's enough evidence to convict Jesus Christ of being a healer, prophet, priest, and the divine Son of God.

The Biblical Account
The NEW BIRTH is our spiritual birth into Christ. By asking Jesus Christ to forgive us of our sins, to come into our hearts, and to be the Lord of our lives, we can be "born again."

Born Again?

"Born again" is *not* a trite phrase that turns people off when they hear it. What did Jesus mean when He said those words? Let's look at the biblical account:

There was a man of the Pharisees named Nicodemus, a ruler of the Jews. This man came to Jesus by night and said to Him, "Rabbi, we know that You are a teacher come from God; for no one can do these signs that You do unless God is with him." Jesus answered and said to him, "Most assuredly, I say to you, unless one is born-again, he cannot see the kingdom of God."
Nicodemus said to Him, "How can a man be born when he is old? Can he enter a second time into his mother's womb and be born?" Jesus answered, "Most assuredly, I say to

*you, unless one is born of water
and the Spirit, he cannot enter the
kingdom of God. That which is
born of the flesh is flesh, and
that which is born of the Spirit is
spirit."* John 3:1-6

What Did Jesus Mean?
In this Scripture, Jesus told
Nicodemus that he *must* be born
again. Those words sound strange
to someone who has never heard
them expressed. Think about what
Jesus meant, as we take a look at
several Scriptures.

In 2 Corinthians 5:17 we read
about what Jesus was trying to
explain to Nicodemus: "Therefore
if any man be in Christ, he is a
new creature: old things are
passed away; behold, all things are
become new."

In this scripture, Paul was teaching believers that when they became followers of Christ, a transformation took place.

When you look up the Greek translation for "creation" in *Vine's Expository Dictionary of New Testament Words*, you will find the following definition:

> **Creation as a noun, 2937, ktisis:** *Primarily "the act of creating," or "the creative act in process," as in 2 Corinthians 5:17 "new creation":... and refers is to what the believer is in Christ; in consequence of the creative act he has become a new creature."* * *[*From Notes on Galatians, by Hogg and Vine, p. 339.]*

If any man is in Christ, he is a new creation. Something supernatural takes place. You will be created, built by the Holy Spirit. Jesus' death on the cross has made it possible for you to be "born again."

"Born Again" in the Bible

Jesus answered and said to him, "Most assuredly, I say to you, unless one is born again, he cannot see the kingdom of God." John 3:3

Do not marvel that I said to you, "You must be born again." John 3:7

...Having been born again, not of corruptible seed but incorruptible, through the word of God which lives and abides forever. 1 Peter 1:23

Prescription for Peace

1. *Start with today.*

2. *Think about God's love for you.*

3. *The words "new creation" in the Bible, where it describes the new birth, mean "new species" from the Greek.*

4. *God is the God of new things.*

5. *He is the Lord of new things for you.*

6. *What He has done for someone else He can do for you.*
   Romans 2:11; Ephesians 6:9

CHAPTER TWO

Journey of Peace...
MIRACLE-WORKING GOD

Through this book, you are going to begin a journey toward peace. While this book is not intended to portray a medical healing or psychological cure, it will lead you to the Creator of the universe and to the One who created the heart, mind, soul, and emotions in the first place.

This is a book designed to help you to pray for peace and wholeness. It also contains the promises of God that are included in the Bible. First of all, you have God in your life, or have invited Him into your life. You have prayed for Jesus Christ to come into your heart [spirit], forgiving and cleansing you of all sin. You have asked Him to take over...to take control of the leadership of your life and make you into the person He wants you to be. That's a great beginning.

Now what? How can you begin the journey of help, healing, and wholeness in God?

A True Account
I know a person (I will call her Mary) who suffered trauma. After it all took place, Mary began to hear voices, and cursing, and she actually felt demonic torment, physically. She had a sense of hopelessness and of not wanting to live. She couldn't laugh, cry, or smile. She had stopped leaving her house except for groceries for about sev-

enteen months. Mary called Christian prayer lines, asking for prayer. God was intervening. She went on a three-day [no food or water] fast, desiring God to do the miraculous and to help. Mary was determined to hear from God and she did.

God Answers

The following is only the beginning. After these first instructions, Mary received comfort from God in the midst of her struggles. God revealed to her that He is extremely close to the suffering. What a mighty and wonderful God He is!

Here is what God clearly led Mary to do:

1. Spend time each day telling Him every detail of what she was going through.

2. Let Him be her all. He was the Creator of the human life and personality and He could heal it. He would be Mary's physician and Counselor.

3. Pray without ceasing; praying in the Spirit...and with her understanding. Talk to God during the day and at night when awake.

4. Trust God with everything she was going through, resting on His Word. Do as the Shunamite woman who, when the prophet of God asked her how it was with her, said, "It shall be well." God Himself could do a work and there is nothing too hard for Him. Mary went about her home saying:

"I believe God; God is able; God is fighting my battles; He which has begun a good work in me will per-

form it to the day of Jesus Christ."
The Word of God is the Sword of
the Spirit.

5. Read the promises of God and
   meditate on them.

God Sends Help
Mary privately told God that there
was only one woman in whom she
trusted, who He could send to help
her. In September of 1976 that
woman drove into Mary's driveway
and got out of the car. Mary came to
the door.

The woman said: "God has sent
me; can I come in?" Of course she let
her in. This woman took Mary to a
church meeting that was going on
about eighty miles away.

At the Church...
As Mary sat in that church, the meeting began with a song: "He Reached

Out His Hand for Me..." When the singing was done, the preacher came out, stopped, and looked at Mary and said, "You've been living, in, like a prison for a long time. This is your night.
You've been mistreated [she had been]."

That is a demonstration of the gifts of the Spirit. This was only the beginning for Mary. She continued her prayer life. Although it was gradual, she was healed, no longer heard voices, or suffered the severe torment.

Mary understands fully the power of the Living Christ to heal a life!

One day Mary sat in on a Bible school class. As she sat there, the power of the Holy Spirit came upon her, saturating her with knowledge: "Sit in on these classes and let My

Word heal you." There was healing and life in God's Word. She has since gone on to earn a BA in Biblical Studies. She couldn't get enough of God's living Word. She has a fruitful and whole life today. She still spends time with the Lord, knowing for herself of His limitless power. He revealed Mary the healing in the Word of God written about in Proverbs 4:20-22.

Noted revivalist, Leonard Ravenhill once said he didn't even want to go to a church where the preacher doesn't spend a lot of time in prayer.

Go online and listen to "Revival Hymn" at www.sermonindex.com. Leonard must have found out what Mary now knew. There has to be and is a difference in a person who spends a lot of time in the presence of God.

Talk to God or Man?
Although God should be the first one we "tell all" to, if you can find a Holy Spirit-filled counselor, he or she will pray with us and share His Word with us, and then it is God Who heals by His Spirit. If you have a counselor, you should also tell your story to him! God can help you. He gave us *people* in the body of Christ.

If you are seeing a psychologist, psychiatrist, or counselor, don't stop. If a doctor has prescribed medication for you, don't stop taking it. God is not limited and can heal you and improve

your well-being no matter what.
God also uses man.

I recently attended a Billy
Graham "His Presence in Crisis
Training" class. Dr. Jonathan
Olford, Psy.D., FPPPR, Crisis and
Consultation Services
International was the main speak-
er at the training sessions. He
spoke of the importance and
value of letting people tell their
story.

The seventeen months Mary
shut herself up, Christian radio
and television preachers were her
church.

God was the Person she talked
to. She told God everything every
day. You should do the same. It
may be a very gradual process,
but there is hope.

Were you a victim or a sinner? He cares and is able to help. There is nothing too difficult for God. Allow the Holy Spirit to be your Comforter.

God is a healer. Set your gaze on what's ahead...with hope!

Prescription for Peace

1. *Ask GOD to grant healing and peace and comfort through your need or trauma... on to help and healing.*

2. *God is more than able to help you.*

CHAPTER THREE

Eyes Forward...

YESTERDAY IS PAST

Dear God,
I cannot heal my mind, heart, emotions,
or body. I entrust my whole being into
Your hands. I ask you to lead me through
this process. I ask You to immerse my
spirit, soul, mind, and body with Your
healing power. Please grant healing to
me, God, according to Your sovereign
plan. Grant me the grace and power for
a new attitude, a new heart, and hold
me up above the suffering. Grant grace to
forget the past and to look forward.
Grant healing to every part of my being
that has been exposed to things that
have required the need for this healing.
Thank You for your kindness and
limitless power.

Your Future

Try to stop dwelling on the past. You may be suffering severely, right now, but God *is not limited* and can extend His power and grace toward you in this need, *now.*

What Should I Think About?

What you need to do is think about the fact that the future is in *front* of you. Think about how God is able to comfort you, help you, and restore you. Think about this:

Behold, I am the Lord, the God of all flesh. Is there anything too hard for Me? Jeremiah 32:27

Is there anything too hard for an almighty, limitless God? God CAN help you. God cares for you. Look what Paul the apostle wrote:

Brethren, I do not count myself to have apprehended; but one thing I

*do, **forgetting those things which are behind** and reaching forward to those things which are ahead.*
Philippians 3:3 (emphasis added)

Why have I placed Scripture in this book? I'll tell you why. Years ago, during the Jesus Movement, people all around were using drugs. One night, two guys and a girl were on a mountainside and experiencing an LSD trip. They all saw the same thing at the same time: a huge starry sky, then two hands roll the sky up like a scroll and the stars flee away.

The young woman started screaming because her father was a preacher, and she recognized the vision as part of a prophecy in the book of Revelation. This prophecy was describing the last days.

Later, bunches of kids started committing their lives to Jesus Christ. They noticed that simply by reading the Scriptures their minds were being healed.

"My son, give attention to my words; Incline your ear to my sayings. Do not let them depart from your eyes; Keep them in the midst of your heart; For they are life to those who find them, and health to all their flesh."
Proverbs 4:20-22

Prescription for Peace

1. *Tell Him you want Him in your future. Meet with Him each day to tell Him all.*
2. *There is nothing too hard for Him.*

CHAPTER FOUR

Help & Comfort
FROM THE HOLY SPIRIT

Dear Lord God,
Hold me up above the difficulties I
am experiencing. I ask You to hide
me under the shadow of Your wings
(Psalm 91) and in Your high tower
(Psalm 144:2). You are El Shaddai,
the All-Sufficient One. Your Word
tells those who suffer to commit
themselves and their souls to You
(1 Peter 4:19). I right now place
my spirit, soul, mind, and body into
Your hands. I am asking You for Your
peace and not that of the world...a
supernatural peace. I trust You to be
my healer, comforter, and strength,
and ask for it in Jesus' name.

~Scriptural Confirmation~

"For the mountains shall depart and the hills be removed, but My kindness shall not depart from you, nor shall My covenant of peace be removed," says the Lord, who has mercy on you.
Isaiah 54:10

The Lord will give strength to His people; the Lord will bless His people with peace. Psalm 29:11

Great peace have those who love Your law, and nothing causes them to stumble. Psalm 119:165

Behold, God is my salvation, I will trust and not be afraid; for Yah, the Lord, is my strength and song; He also has become my salvation. Isaiah 12:2

Be of good courage, and He shall strengthen your heart, all you who hope in the Lord. Psalm 31:24

O God, You are more awesome than Your holy places. The God of Israel is He who gives strength and power to His people. Blessed be God! Psalm 68:35

But the Lord will be a shelter for His people, and the strength of the children of Israel. Joel 3:16

For God has not given us a spirit of fear, but of power and of love and of a sound mind. 2 Timothy 1:7

For His merciful kindness is great toward us, and the truth of the Lord endures forever. Praise the Lord! Psalm 117:2

Let, I pray, Your merciful kindness be for my comfort, according to Your word to Your servant. Psalm 119:76

Then they cried out to the Lord in their trouble, and He saved them out of their distresses. Psalm 107:19

Prescription for Peace

❧

1. *Pray for help to forget the past. Remember that your future is "in front" of you.*

2. *God is able to help you, comfort you, heal you, and restore you.*

3. *God loves you.*

4. *Tell Him everything, although He already knows it.*

CHAPTER FIVE

In His Path
IS PEACE

*Dear God,
Guide my footsteps in Your Word and
let no iniquity have dominion over me.
Lead me by Your Holy Spirit. Enlighten
my darkness. Cause me to walk in the
right path for Your name's sake. Lead
me in Your truth and teach me. In Your
path is peace. Fill my mind, heart, and
soul with Your peace. Direct my steps
in Your wisdom. The Bible says that if
I ask anything according to Your will,
You hear me and I can have the petitions I ask of You (1 John 5:14).
I thank You, in advance, for what You
are doing and are going to do, in Jesus'
name. Amen.*

~Scriptural Confirmation~

*He restores my soul; He leads me in
the paths of righteousness for His
name's sake.* Psalm 23:3

*They shall neither hunger nor thirst,
neither heat nor sun shall strike them;
for He Who has mercy on them will
lead them, even by the springs of water
He will guide them.* Isaiah 49:10

*For this is God, our God forever and
ever; He will be our guide even to
death.* Psalm 48:14

*You will guide me with Your counsel,
and afterward receive me to glory.*
Psalm 73:24

*In all your ways acknowledge Him, and
He shall direct your paths.* Proverbs 3:6

*A man's heart plans his way, but the
Lord directs his steps.* Proverbs 16:9

I will bring the blind by a way they did not know; I will lead them in paths they have not known. I will make darkness light before them, and crooked places straight. These things I will do for them, and not forsake them. Isaiah 42:16

Your ears shall hear a word behind you, saying, "This is the way, walk in it," whenever you turn to the right hand or whenever you turn to the left. Isaiah 30:21

The Lord will guide you continually, and satisfy your soul in drought, and strengthen your bones; you shall be like a watered garden, and like a spring of water, whose waters do not fail. Isaiah 58:11

However, when He, the Spirit of truth, has come, He will guide you into all truth; for He will not speak on His own authority, but whatever He hears He will speak; and He will tell you things to come. John 16:13

Prescription for Peace

1. *God loves all people.*
2. *God loves me.*
3. *God can help me.*
4. *If I ask for help, He will help me.*
5. *He has helped me even when I have not asked!*

CHAPTER SIX

Divine Protection

PSALM 91

*Dear Heavenly Father,
I ask for Your divine protection for
me and my brothers and sisters.
Send Your army of angels and
chariots of fire to fight battles.
Protect me, in Jesus' name. You hold
the heavens and the earth in Your
hands, and even if the earth were
removed and the mountains be cast
into the sea, I will not fear, for You
are with me. There is nothing too
hard for You. If I dwell in the secret
place of the Most High, I abide under
the shadow of the Almighty. Under
Your shadow I take refuge. I commit
myself into Your care, in Jesus'
name, amen.*

He who dwells in the secret place of the Most High shall abide under the shadow of the Almighty. I will say of the Lord, "He is my refuge and my fortress; My God, in Him I will trust." He shall cover you with His feathers, and under His wings you shall take refuge; His truth shall be your shield and buckler. No evil shall befall you, nor shall any plague come near your dwelling.
Psalm 91:1, 2, 4, 10

I will both lie down in peace, and sleep; For You alone, O Lord, make me dwell in safety. Psalm 4:8

But whoever listens to me will dwell safely, and will be secure, without fear of evil. Proverbs 1:33

The name of the Lord is a strong tower; the righteous run to it and are safe. Proverbs 18:10

The Lord shall preserve you from all evil; He shall preserve your soul. The Lord shall preserve your going out and your coming in from this time forth, and even forevermore. Psalms 121:7–8

But now, thus says the Lord, who created you, O Jacob, and He who formed you, O Israel: "Fear not, for I have redeemed you; I have called you by your name; you are Mine. When you pass through the waters, I will be with you; and through the rivers, they shall not overflow you. When you walk through the fire, you shall not be burned, nor shall the flame scorch you. Isaiah 43:1–2

Prescription for Peace

1. Meditating on God's Word brings health and healing to "all MY flesh..."

2. It says this in Proverbs 4:20. If God's Word says it...that settles it!

3. His Word is like medicine to me!

CHAPTER SEVEN

Let God Fight

YOUR BATTLES

Lord God,
I thank You for all You have done for
me. I praise You for Your kindness and
mercy upon me. Abide with me, Lord.
Draw me close to You by Your Holy
Spirit. You alone possess all power in
heaven and in earth, and there is
nothing too hard for You. I come to
You in Jesus' name, Father, and I ask
You, to fight the spiritual battle I am
experiencing. You alone possess the
power to destroy the works of darkness
or to heal and comfort those who suf-
fer. Defeat them that fight against me.
You are fair and good to all who call
upon You. I ask Your help, in Jesus'
name. Amen.

~ Scriptural Confirmation ~

And Asa cried out to the Lord his God, and said, "Lord, it is nothing for You to help, whether with many or with those who have no power; help us, O Lord our God, for we rest on You, and in Your name we go against this multitude. O Lord, You are our God; do not let man prevail against You!" 2 Chronicles 14:11

Many are the afflictions of the righteous, but the Lord delivers him out of them all. Psalm 34:19

Though I walk in the midst of trouble, You will revive me; You will stretch out Your hand against the wrath of my enemies, and Your right hand will save me. Psalm 138:7

Then they cried out to the Lord in their trouble, and He saved them out of their distresses. Psalm 107:19

"Indeed they shall surely assemble, but not because of Me. Whoever assembles against you shall fall for your sake. No weapon formed against you shall prosper, and every tongue which rises against you in judgment you shall condemn. This is the heritage of the servants of the Lord, and their righteousness is from Me," says the Lord. Isaiah 54:15, 17

The Lord will cause your enemies who rise against you to be defeated before your face; they shall come out against you one way and flee before you seven ways. Deuteronomy 28:7

Through God we will do valiantly, for it is He who shall tread down our enemies. Psalm 60:12

Those who war against you shall be as nothing, as a nonexistent thing. Isaiah 41:12

Prescription for Peace

1. *God loves me.*
2. *God is my Protector.*
3. *God is my Guard.*
4. *He is my Shield and High Tower.*
5. *He possesses ALL power!*

CHAPTER EIGHT

Divine Provision

FOR YOUR NEEDS

Dear Heavenly Father,
I ask for You to provide for my natural, physical, and spiritual needs in Jesus' name. I need You, Lord, and look to You. I know that in the Scriptures, You performed miracles. I believe You are limitless in power today. Jesus fed a multitude with a few loaves and fishes. In Philippians 4:19, Your Word says that You will provide for all of our needs according to Your riches in glory by Christ Jesus. I rest my faith in You, in Your integrity, and in the integrity of the Scriptures, and I thank You for what You are going to do, in Jesus' name.

The Lord is my shepherd; I shall not want. You prepare a table before me in the presence of my enemies; You anoint my head with oil; my cup runs over. Psalm 23:1, 5

But seek first the kingdom of God and His righteousness, and all these things shall be added to you. Matthew 6:33

And my God shall supply all your need according to His riches in glory by Christ Jesus. Philippians 4:19

Trust in the Lord, and do good; dwell in the land, and feed on His faithfulness. Psalm 37:3

He has given food to those who fear Him; He will ever be mindful of His covenant. Psalm 111:5

*He makes peace in your borders, and
fills you with the finest wheat.*
Psalm 147:14

*The righteous eats to the satisfying
of his soul, but the stomach of the
wicked shall be in want.*
Proverbs 13:25

*Look at the birds of the air, for they
neither sow nor reap nor gather into
barns; yet your heavenly Father feeds
them. Are you not of more value
than they?* Matthew 6:26

*Therefore I say to you, do not worry
about your life, what you will eat or
what you will drink; nor about your
body, what you will put on. Is not
life more than food and the body
more than clothing? Now if God so
clothes the grass of the field, which
today is, and tomorrow is thrown*

into the oven, will He not much more clothe you, O you of little faith? Therefore do not worry, saying, "What shall we eat?" or "What shall we drink?" or "What shall we wear?" For after all these things the Gentiles seek. For your heavenly Father knows that you need all these things.

Matthew 6:25, 30, 31, 32

Prescription for Peace

1. *God cares for me.*
2. *God is my Provider.*
3. *God can meet my needs.*

CHAPTER NINE

Be Made Whole:

ACCEPT FORGIVENESS

Dear God,
I ask that You breathe Your breath of
life into me. Miracles exist today.
You are a present help in the time of
trouble. I ask you for the forgiveness
of all of my sins. I also accept your
forgiveness. Grant healing and cause
the healing power of Jesus to fill my
body, mind, soul, and spirit. You are
Jehovah Rapha (the Lord that heals)
and I ask for healing in Jesus' name.
Thank You, God, that You are limit-
less in power and might. Thank You
that you care for me and my friends,
and for touching me by Your Holy
Spirit, right now. I rest my faith and
hope in You, in Your power, and in
Your Word and promises.

~ Scriptural Confirmation ~

Bless the Lord...Who forgives all your iniquities, Who heals all your diseases, Who redeems your life from destruction, Who crowns you with lovingkindness and tender mercies, Who satisfies your mouth with good things, and that your youth is renewed like the eagle's.
Psalm 103:3-5

He sent His word and healed them, and delivered them from their destructions. Psalm 107:20

For they are life to those who find them, and health to all their flesh.
Proverbs 4:22

So you shall serve the Lord your God, and He will bless your bread and your water. And I will take sickness

away from the midst of you.
Exodus 23:25

If you diligently heed the voice of the Lord your God and do what is right in His sight, give ear to His commandments and keep all His statutes, I will put none of the diseases on you which I have brought on the Egyptians. For I am the Lord who heals you. Exodus 15:26

Behold, I will bring it health and healing; I will heal them and reveal to them the abundance of peace and truth. Jeremiah 33:6

The Spirit of the Lord is upon Me [it IS upon Jesus, your healer], because He has anointed Me to preach the gospel to the poor; He has sent Me to heal the brokenhearted, to preach

deliverance to the captives and
recovery of sight to the blind, to set
at liberty those who are oppressed.
Luke 4:18

Prescription for Peace

1. *Forgive all who have wronged you.*
2. *Receive forgiveness from God after asking for that forgiveness.*
3. *Keep your eyes on God... His integrity...His Word... His power.*

CHAPTER TEN

Help Me Now

BY YOUR GRACE

Heavenly Father,
I can't handle this situation. Touch
my mind by Your Holy Spirit, Father.
Heal and comfort my mind and emo-
tions. Hold me up above these things I
am experiencing, as I cannot handle
them in my own strength. The Bible
tells us to cast our cares totally on You
and to trust in You for every need (1
Peter 5:7; Phil. 4:19). I turn all of this
pain and turmoil over to You right
now, and I am going to trust in Your
help for all of this. Grant supernatural
peace by Your Holy Spirit, in Jesus'
name. I rest my faith in Your promis-
es. I will now thank You for what You
are going to do. Amen.

~Scriptural Confirmation~

Therefore humble yourselves under the mighty hand of God, that He may exalt you in due time, casting all your care upon Him, for He cares for you. 1 Peter 5:6–7

And my God shall supply all your need according to His riches in glory by Christ Jesus. Philippians 4:19

Then they cried out to the Lord in their trouble, and He saved them out of their distresses. Psalm 107:19

The righteous is delivered from trouble, and it comes to the wicked instead. Proverbs 11:8

For I know the thoughts that I think toward you, says the Lord, thoughts of peace and not of evil, to give you a future and a hope. Jeremiah 29:11

*Then shall the virgin rejoice in the
dance, and the young men and the old,
together; for I will turn their mourning
to joy, will comfort them, and make
them rejoice rather than sorrow.*
Jeremiah 31:13

*The Lord also will be a refuge for the
oppressed, a refuge in times of trouble.*
Psalm 9:9

*Wait on the Lord; be of good courage,
and He shall strengthen your heart;
wait, I say, on the Lord!*
Psalm 27:10, 14

*God is our refuge and strength, a very
present help in trouble. Therefore we
will not fear, even though the earth be
removed, and though the mountains be
carried into the midst of the sea; though
its waters roar and be troubled, though*

the mountains shake with its
swelling. Psalm 46:1-3

Prescription for Peace

1. *God is a present help in my*
   trouble.
2. *I can ask Him to help me,*
   and He will help me!
3. *He is MY God.*
4. *He cares for me (1 Peter 5:7).*

CHAPTER ELEVEN

Hidden in God...

UNDER HIS WINGS

Dear Lord God,
I ask You to hide me in You. He who
dwells in the secret place of the Most
High shall abide under the shadow
of the Almighty (Psalm 91:1). Keep
me as the apple of Your eye; hide me
under the shadow of Your wings
(Psalm 36:7). I place my spirit, soul,
mind, and body into Your hands.
You alone are God. You alone can
heal me. Jesus said, "I am the resur-
rection and the life. He who believes
in Me, though he may die, he shall
live." If any man believe in You,
Jesus, though He were dead yet shall
he live..." (John 11:25). Be my heal-
er, comforter, and strength in Jesus'
name. Amen.

I will give peace in the land, and you shall lie down, and none will make you afraid; I will rid the land of evil beasts, and the sword will not go through your land. Leviticus 26:6

The Lord will give strength to His people; the Lord will bless His people with peace. Psalm 29:11

Great peace have those who love Your law, and nothing causes them to stumble. Psalm 119:165

He gives power to the weak, and to those who have no might He increases strength. Even the youths shall faint and be weary, and the young men shall utterly fall, but those who wait on the Lord shall renew their strength; they shall mount up with wings like eagles, they shall run and not be weary, they shall walk and not faint. Isaiah 40:29-31

And He said to me, "My grace is sufficient for you, for My strength is made perfect in weakness." Therefore most gladly I will rather boast in my infirmities, that the power of Christ may rest upon me. 2 Corinthians 12:9

Be of good courage, and He shall strengthen your heart, all you who hope in the Lord. Psalm 31:24

O God, You are more awesome than Your holy places. The God of Israel is He who gives strength and power to His people. Blessed be God! Psalm 68:35

But the Lord will be a shelter for His people, and the strength of the children of Israel. Joel 3:16

For God has not given us a spirit of fear, but of power and of love and of a sound mind. 2 Timothy 1:7

Prescription for Peace

1. I am hidden in Christ.
2. I am blessed by His Spirit.
3. I am under His mighty wings.

CHAPTER TWELVE

Why, Lord?

WHOLE IN CHRIST

Lord Jesus,
I have asked for forgiveness for all of
my sins. You have heard me and for-
given me. Still, I ask You: "Why did
this happen to me? Why did this
happen to my friend(s)?" Please heal
my heart and remove all sorrow and
condemnation from me. You are able
to remove these guilty feelings from
me. Redirect my feelings toward
compassion for others and for those
who are in need around me, in Jesus'
name. Although I do not understand
fully, I know You know all things,
and I commit it all into Your hands.
Surround us all with Your grace.
Thank You, for Your help, kindness,
and tender mercies toward us. Amen.

So we may boldly say: "The Lord is my helper; I will not fear. What can man do to me?" Hebrews 13:6

So you shall serve the Lord your God, and He will bless your bread and your water. And I will take sickness away from the midst of you. Exodus 23:25

He who dwells in the secret place of the Most High shall abide under the shadow of the Almighty. I will say of the Lord, "He is my refuge and my fortress; my God, in Him I will trust." Surely He shall deliver you from the snare of the fowler and from the perilous pestilence. He shall cover you with His feathers, and under His wings you shall take refuge; His truth shall be your shield and buckler. You shall not be afraid of the terror by night, nor of the arrow

*that flies by day, nor of the pestilence
that walks in darkness, nor of the
destruction that lays waste at noonday.
A thousand may fall at your side, and
ten thousand at your right hand; but it
shall not come near you. Only with
your eyes shall you look, and see the
reward of the wicked. Because you have
made the Lord, who is my refuge, even
the Most High, your dwelling place, no
evil shall befall you, nor shall any
plague come near your dwelling; for He
shall give His angels charge over you, to
keep you in all your ways.*
Psalm 91:1-11

*Who forgives all your iniquities, Who
heals all your diseases.* Psalm 103:3

*The Lord will strengthen him on his
bed of illness; You will sustain him on
his sickbed.* Psalm 41:3

"Then shall the virgin rejoice in the dance, and the young men and the old, together; for I will turn their mourning to joy, will comfort them, and make them rejoice rather than sorrow."
Jeremiah 31:13

Prescription for Peace

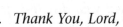

1. *Thank You, Lord, for Your wonderful forgiveness and grace.*

2. *I will now wait before You, thinking about Your Word, thanking You for your kindness, love, peace, and for the help You have given me.*

Comfort My Friends

& OUR FAMILIES

Dear God,
Please comfort the hearts of my friends and their families. Hold them up above any pain and in Your heavenly peace. My heart has also been broken. Send Your Holy Spirit to comfort us. Thank You for being with each one. Please grant the grace to remember that death is a temporary separation. We shall all be together for eternity with You, through salvation in Jesus Christ. Grant us the mercy and grace to live in Your grace. I ask all of these things in Jesus' name, amen.

For I am persuaded that neither death nor life, nor angels nor principalities nor powers, nor things present nor things to come, nor height nor depth, nor any other created thing, shall be able to separate us from the love of God which is in Christ Jesus our Lord.
Romans 8:38, 39

Yea, though I walk through the valley of the shadow of death, I will fear no evil; for You are with me; Your rod and Your staff, they comfort me.
Psalm 23:4

For in the time of trouble He shall hide me in His pavilion; in the secret place of His tabernacle He shall hide me; He shall set me high upon a rock. And now my head shall be lifted up above my enemies all around me;

*therefore I will offer sacrifices of joy
in His tabernacle; I will sing, yes, I
will sing praises to the Lord.*
Psalm 27:5, 6

*So he answered, "Do not fear, for
those who are with us are more
than those who are with them."*
2 Kings 6:16

*"I know the thoughts that I think
toward you," saith the* LORD,
*"thoughts of peace, and not of evil,
to give you an expected end."*
Jeremiah 29:11

*He heals the brokenhearted, and
binds up their wounds.*
Psalm 147:3

*He shall give his angels charge over
you, to keep you in all your ways.
They shall bear you up in their*

hands, lest you dash your foot against a stone. Psalm 91:11, 12

Let the peace of God rule in your hearts, to which also you were called in one body, and be thankful.
Colossians 3:15

Peace I leave with you, My peace I give to you: not as the world gives do I give to you. John 14:27

Prescription for Peace

1. *I will start fresh each day.*
2. *I will look to the Lord.*
3. *I will hope in the Lord.*
4. *I will praise and thank Him.*

Part Two

Prayer Study & Promises

Lord of Victory

FOR ALL MY LIFE

Spiritual battles are won when we take everything to God. In fact, God can do everything, anything, and all things...HE is limitless.

Ephesians 6:18 says, "praying always with all prayer and supplication in the Spirit..." This says it all.

What does all prayer include? It includes thanksgiving, praise, worship, prayer in the Spirit, supplication, and standing on specific promises (the Amplified Bible describes it as resting the whole of our confidence and trust on God). In fact, don't worry if you don't know how to pray for hours or perfectly right. You can sit with the Lord and talk to Him as a friend while you learn how to pray the way the Bible teaches.

Unless God specifically leads you to address the devil, don't. Keep your focus on the Lord and on what He has called you to do. Ask God to fight your spiritual battles in Jesus' name and trust in His power.

For we do not wrestle against flesh and blood, but against principalities, against powers, against the rulers of the darkness of this age, against spiritual hosts of wickedness in the heavenly places. Ephesians 6:12

In this life there is a very real battle going on. God's Word contains spiritual weapons. In the book of Ephesians, when Paul is teaching the body of Christ about their armor, he says:

And take the helmet of salvation, and the sword of the Spirit which is the Word of God; praying always with all prayer and supplication in the Spirit, being watchful to this end with all perseverance and supplication for all the saints. Ephesians 6:17–18

Use the Sword of the Word

Learn to apply and use the Word of God properly. It is like the difference between children who play at sword fighting and a swordsman who, after much training, has developed his skill. He is a master at what he does. The muscles he uses have become developed and strong. He has become quick, and when he strikes with the sword, he hits his target forcefully.

It won't happen overnight, but after growing and developing spiritually, we can become master swordsmen with the Word of God! There is supernatural power in the Word of God. It is spiritual food, and it is the sword of the Spirit. The enemy must flee at the name of Jesus, and God's Word is a weapon.

Having disarmed principalities and powers, He made a public spectacle of them, triumphing over them in it. Colossians 2:15

Jesus stood on Scripture when He faced temptation (Matthew 4). The very Word of God proceeded from His mouth. The Word of God is the sword of the Spirit.

The Sword in Prayer

Another of the great spiritual weapons in God is written about in Scripture: "...praying always with all prayer and supplication in the Spirit" (Eph. 6:18). Praying in the Spirit is a supernatural weapon.

One example of prayer using the Sword of the Spirit follows:

Father, Your Word says in Psalm 27 that You are the strength of my life. I thank You for it! You show no partiality (Acts 10:34). Your Word says that You are able to do more than I can ask or even think (Ephesians 3:20). There is nothing too hard for You (Jeremiah 32:17). You are the Mighty God, limitless in power (Deuteronomy 4:34; 7:19). Your Word will not return

void (Isaiah 55:11)! I ask you to
[your request] in Jesus' name
(John 14:14, 16), and I praise You
for what You are doing in my life
(or in the life of the person for
whom you are praying).

Can you find the Scriptures
within the above prayer? I have ref-
erenced the words that contained
Scripture. Jesus has already defeated
Satan for you through His redemp-
tive work of the cross. We make
this living reality through prayer
and by the appropriation of God's
Word and promises for our own
lives (2 Corinthians 10:4;
1 Peter 5:9). What an adventure!

CHAPTER FIFTEEN

Prayer Power:

GOD S POWER

God is alive now. He has love beyond our comprehension. Just think about that. He IS love. Finding that out will change your life forever. Knowing how great and powerful He is, and reading the following verses, will refresh you and revive that fact.

Second Chronicles 20:12–22 tells the story of the prophet Johaz. The Spirit of the Lord told him to tell the people not be afraid of the great multitude who were coming against them. It was the Lord's battle and not theirs. When they began to sing and to praise, the Lord caused an ambush against their enemies. This is an exciting example of what God can do when we look to Him, worship Him, and praise Him! Read the Scripture:

"O our God, will You not judge them? For we have no power against this great multitude that is coming against us; nor do we know what to do, but our eyes are upon You." Now all Judah, with their little ones, their wives, and their children, stood before the LORD. Then the Spirit of the LORD came upon Jahaziel the son of Zechariah, the son of Benaiah, the son of Jeiel, the son of Mattaniah, a Levite of the sons of Asaph, in the midst of the assembly. And he said, "Listen, all you of Judah and you inhabitants of Jerusalem, and

you, King Jehoshaphat! Thus says the LORD *to you: 'Do not be afraid nor dismayed because of this great multitude, for the battle is not yours, but God's. Tomorrow go down against them. They will surely come up by the Ascent of Ziz, and you will find them at the end of the brook before the Wilderness of Jeruel. You will not need to fight in this battle. Position yourselves, stand still and see the salvation of the* LORD*, who is with you, O Judah and Jerusalem!' Do not fear or be dismayed; tomorrow go out against them, for the* LORD *is with you." And Jehoshaphat bowed his head with his face to the ground, and all Judah and the inhabitants of Jerusalem bowed before the* LORD*, worshiping the* LORD*. Then the*

*Levites of the children of the
Kohathites and of the children of
the Korahites stood up to praise the
Lord God of Israel with voices
loud and high. So they rose early in
the morning and went out into the
Wilderness of Tekoa; and as they
went out, Jehoshaphat stood and
said, "Hear me, O Judah and you
inhabitants of Jerusalem: Believe
in the Lord your God, and you
shall be established; believe His
prophets, and you shall prosper."
And when he had consulted with
the people, he appointed those who
should sing to the Lord, and who
should praise the beauty of holi-
ness, as they went out before the
army and were saying: "Praise the
Lord, for His mercy endures forever." Now when they began to sing
and to praise, the Lord set*

*ambushes against the
people of Ammon, Moab, and Mount
Seir, who had come against Judah;
and they were defeated.*
2 Chronicles 20:12–22

Prayers of the Spirit

When we pray in the Spirit, the
Holy Spirit takes over, praying
through us according to God's will.
The following Scriptures mention
this kind of prayer:

*Likewise the Spirit also helps in our
weaknesses. For we do not know what
we should pray for as we ought, but
the Spirit Himself makes intercession
for us with groanings which cannot
be uttered.* Romans 8:26

*But you, beloved, building yourselves
up on your most holy faith, praying
in the Holy Spirit...* Jude 20

Waiting in God's Presence

Waiting in the presence of God is an extremely effective type of prayer that always brings huge results. I know it for a fact....

While attending Bible college, I had a remarkable experience that I want to share with you. This experience will help you to understand what this type of praying can do.

One of my teachers was an intercessor who shared a valuable insight with the class. He told us that the most powerful kind of prayer was waiting in the presence of God on behalf of someone or some situation. He said he didn't know why it was so powerful, but his experience had proven it to be so. I just listened and wondered about it.

"Mom" Goodwin

I left class that day to drive to
Mom Goodwin's house. She was
my spiritual mother, living in
Broken Arrow, Oklahoma, at the
time. She had moved there after
her husband went home to be with
the Lord. She and her husband,
Rev. J. R. Goodwin, were pastors for
forty-eight years in the same little
church in Texas. They were written
about in many books. They knew
about the moving of the Holy
Spirit.

Mom had a ministry of intercession. When she had a dream,
vision, or word of knowledge about
a person or event, she would pray
about it. In the next few days the
answers to her prayers would come
to pass in the lives of those for

whom she had prayed. This was a proven, sound manifestation of the Holy Spirit operating in her life.

The Goodwins were also known for their counseling of ministers who often made it a point to travel to visit with them. When they all prayed, God always confirmed, through Mom and Dad Goodwin, what He had been leading and speaking to those visiting ministers. Dad Goodwin was a stickler for the Word. He taught the verse-by-verse method.

Frequently, I went to mom's house to work around the house or for fellowship and prayer. We spent many hours together. My association with Mom Goodwin was a special blessing to my life.

While driving to Mom's house, twice this thought came to mind: "Jennie and John [fictional names] can't get out of the Middle East. If someone would wait in God's presence on their behalf, God could get them out of the country." Mind you, I didn't know they couldn't get out of Jordan.

I pulled into the driveway, got out of the car, and walked up to the door where Mom met me. Before I even stepped inside, she said these words, "I just got a call from Voralee—I used to rent from her while in Bible school—and she got a letter from Jennie who says they still can't get out of the Middle East."

I said, "Mom, you won't believe what just happened while

driving over here." I told her about the Bible teaching on prayer and about the thoughts that came to me on my way to her house.

"That sounds like God to me. You better do it," she said.

I was amazed. That night I sat in the presence of God on their behalf. I had sought the Lord many times, but this time I just sat there feeling foolish and thinking: *You are the mighty God...I am nothing.*

I wondered, *Should I read a Scripture? Do I do anything?*

I pretty much just sat there in the presence of God, wondering what I should do. I didn't feel anything.

In two days I got word that my friends gained legal permission to leave the Middle East.

God moved when I waited in His presence. While I'm confident God uses many people and many prayers, in this instance the test for whether it was of God was whether or not what God said came to pass. This was God's Spirit speaking to me. Everything that God said would happen came to pass when I prayed as He directed me to pray.

The Next Year

Almost a year to the date, Jennie and John told me that John's brother (who lived in the Middle East) wanted to come to the United States to go to school but had been turned down eleven times by various European countries and by the U.S.

The next morning I had a dream before waking: I felt an intense love

in my heart. Then I heard myself
speaking to John, "John, I will
pray. God can get your brother
out of the country." I awoke
with that.

"What will John think if I tell
him that? What if that wasn't the
Lord?" I thought about it for
quite a while with mixed feelings
of excitement, wonder, and con-
cern. I knew God could do this.
The experience was mixed with a
tremendous amount of love and
the knowledge that God had done
it for my friends a year earlier. I
decided to be careful how I said it,
but that I would go and tell them
that night.

"John," I began, "I'll pray.
God can get your brother out of
the country."

"Oh, thank you," he said.

That was it! I went home and did it. I guess I spent about an hour waiting in God's presence. I also spent a little time the next day, hoping to feel like I was "done" waiting in His presence for the need.

In two days, permission was granted for my friend's brother to come to the U.S.

Through this kind of prayer God moves mountains; binds the enemy; overthrows the powers of darkness; sends His mighty, heavenly armies; and subdues the enemy in situations. I don't know why it is so powerful. Maybe part of it is spending that time with Him. *He is high and lifted up, while you are the helpless one coming to Him.*

When all hope seems gone and you don't know what to do, wait in God's presence on behalf of the situation.

Miracles in Spain

More recently, my youngest son took a trip to Spain with just his backpack to "live off the land." I prayed all the way through it, and there were many day-to-day miracles. Just before he came back to this country, some interesting events took place. Here is the condensed version:

Two mornings in a row I woke around 4 AM to pray. I felt led by the Holy Spirit to wait in God's presence on his behalf. Each day, there were specific things I felt I to share with my son.

The first morning I felt led to tell my son about an experience I had when I was his age. God caused deep feelings within me that I should not go a certain direction. I had a horrible feeling about taking that direction.

For almost a month those intense feelings came and went. I had never experienced anything like it and didn't know what to make of it. I couldn't figure it out. I didn't listen to the "don't do it" feelings, though, and ended up in a bad situation. Because of all that transpired, I realized God Himself had spoken to me.

I told my son about the experience, and that this was the first time God spoke to me in such a way. I didn't even realize God could do such a thing, although I loved Him and cared about God in my life. I wished I had known it was God. I also told my son I would trust his wisdom, and asked him to be sensitive to his gut feelings.

The next morning I woke with the knowledge that I was to pray, and here's what happened: Shortly after I began praying, I felt like I should call my son. If I hadn't called him right at that moment I would have missed him. He was on a train headed toward France.

He said: "I just wanted to tell you that it happened to me. I felt inside of me that I should come home, but I want to test it. Nothing like this has ever happened to me."

I thought, *Oh no...if God wants him home and he's headed toward France, now what?* I was concerned that he might be headed for trouble.

Soon he was out of cell phone reach. I called a few of my prayer partners and asked them to pray, and I went on to work.

The next morning I felt like I should try to call him one more time. He answered his cell phone. He told me he had gotten off the train in France and found somewhere to sleep for the night. *Waking, a feeling came over him that he couldn't do this anymore. He was drained, and felt that this was the end of him trying to "live off the land" in Europe.*

I later knew that it was God's voice speaking to him. God had spoken to my son, even though he wasn't sure it was God speaking.

He got on a plane and came back to Madrid, where he was getting ready to board a plane to New York when he received my second phone call! Thank God he had left money in the bank for a trip home. The moment I called him, he was indeed in calling range (his cell phone was only for Spain).

"I'm so glad you called me," he said. "I was hoping you would. I'm getting on a plane for the United States right now. In fact, if you had waited a minute, we would be taking off and you couldn't have gotten through to me."

My son got on the plane and was soon back at work in the States. Since that time, my son has had an amazing revelation of the reality of Christ. God keeps proving Himself to my boy! His adventures have only begun!

God's Power Displayed

While finishing up this book, a beautiful example of waiting in God's presence took place.

It was four in the morning and I couldn't sleep. I went downstairs, ready to have devotions, when the phone rang. It was a male friend of mine calling from Michigan. "Jimmy is on life support. He's brain dead and on a respirator. They're stopping life support at 11 o'clock."

I couldn't believe it! Our prayer group at church had been praying for this young man. His father said Jimmy had been experiencing sleep apnea and just stopped breathing. I told him that I had gotten up to pray and would pray for his son. I made a couple of calls to prayer partners and began to wait in God's presence. It was two hours earlier where I was.

Around six, I felt something, although I didn't know what it meant and just remained before the Lord. I prayed a few things as I waited, "that God would send his angels to the hospital in Michigan, pour out His Spirit, and if He could minister to Jimmy in his condition, that He would." I asked God that if He could speak to Jimmy even in a coma, that He would.

"Have mercy on him, Lord. Remember him as a child. I ask for your kindness toward him. You are the only One who can help him. Please don't let him die without being ready."

Those prayers are basically all I could think of to pray.

At 8:10 AM, the Scripture came to me, "I am the resurrection and the life. He who believes in Me, though he may die, he shall live. And whoever lives and believes in Me shall never die." (John 11:25–26).

I thought, *I love that Scripture.* I didn't realize what was happening. I felt strongly that God wanted me to stay before Him for Jimmy.

Then, from 8:15 to 8:30 AM the most wonderful thing I've ever experienced happened. God poured out His powerful, supernatural presence on me. I felt His power, the Kingship of Jesus Christ as Lord and God, and was filled with gratitude and worship.

I praised Him with a supernatural awareness of His goodness, kindness, and compassion. It was a wonderful experience!

"How wonderful God was to Jimmy. God is Almighty. He is so great!"

Jesus had filled my being with *true worship*...I wept for joy. I had joy I had never before experienced in my Spirit. It was great. I *knew* Jimmy was okay. There were now only thirty minutes left before the hospital was going to remove the respirator.

I decided I should stay before the Lord until that time. At eleven Michigan time, a tremendous silent presence of God came over me. I just felt like a child. I thought, *Maybe Jesus and His angels are ready to take Jimmy.*

They were. As the respirator was removed from Jimmy, his dad holding his hand, Jimmy left this life... but stepped into glory with the Lord Jesus.

CHAPTER SIXTEEN

Prayer Workshop:

PEACE & HEALING

This chapter will give you the keys to experiencing results in prayer. It's not a matter of using a key to "get want you want." There is no selfishness involved. I use the word "key" because I found, to my joy, that making a few changes in how I prayed totally regenerated my prayer life and filled my heart and mind with peace.

Be anxious for nothing, but in everything by prayer and supplication, with thanksgiving, let your requests be made known to God; and the peace of God, which surpasses all understanding, will guard your hearts and minds through Christ Jesus. Philippians 4:6–7

The above verse is the theme Scripture for this teaching.

This advice from the apostle Paul sums it up: Don't worry; instead, pray about everything. It then adds that the peace of God, which surpasses understanding, will keep our hearts and minds through Christ Jesus |paraphrased|. What a promise! Of course, we must pray according to God's will and in line with what Scripture teaches us. But many things *are* God's will.

In the Old Testament, David prayed that God would overthrow and overturn the works of darkness, and in response God sent out His arrows and scattered the foe, lightnings in abundance, and

He vanquished them (Psalm 18:14). There are many answers to personal prayers in the Bible. Have you ever wanted to pray but didn't know how to begin? Or have you tried everything but not received the joy and fulfillment you had hoped for in prayer?

Through these steps, you will become renewed in your excitement for spiritual things and about God Himself, His faithfulness, and the integrity of His Word. If you already have received answers, you will be further inspired and become even more full of faith in God. Through spending time with God in prayer, you will experience the priceless treasure of developing a relationship with God.

The price Jesus paid for our sins
at Calvary affords us the opportunity to be born again and to come
into the family of God, which is the
Christian's greatest gift. The relationship we can then have with our
God is the next greatest gift.

Prayer is the key to building a
close relationship with God. As you
engage in prayer, you will never be
the same again.

Prayer need not be tedious. God
does not require you to perform a
list of prerequisites before He will
answer you. Yet there are things that
God asks of us.

Before You Start: Forgiveness
Before you pray, you need to be sure
there is nothing between you and
God. You need to ask for forgiveness
of your sins. You also need to

forgive others of anything you have against them. How can we ask for forgiveness if we refuse to forgive others their trespasses against us (Luke 6:37 and 17:3)?

If I feel like I can't forgive, I ask for *His* help: "God, I can't forgive, but I ask You to love and forgive in and through me by Your Holy Spirit. Please give me the grace." This will work!

Leave your gift there before the altar, and go your way. First be reconciled to your brother, and then come and offer your gift.
Matthew 5:24

Enemies to Answered Prayer
Look at the list of hindrances to prayer below. Take time to pray about these issues in your life. Once you've done it, you will be

more likely to recognize these things as hindrances in your walk with God. You will want to take each issue to God, removing these obstacles from your life as soon as possible:

- Unforgiveness (Matthew 5:24)

- Hatred (Matthew 5:24)

- Doubt (Matthew 17:41; 21:21

  Mark 9:14-29)

- Fear (Matthew 14:30)

- Unconfessed sin (Isaiah 59:2)

Now I will show you how to begin your path to freedom from the burden of unforgiveness.

Noted University Study
Below is an excerpt from *Stanford Medicine,* Volume 16, Number 4, Summer 1999, which is published

quarterly by Stanford University Medical Center:

The Art and Science of Forgiveness

If you feel good but want to feel even better, try forgiving someone.
                    —FREDERIC LUSKIN, PH.D.

For centuries, the world's religious and spiritual traditions have recommended the use of forgiveness as a balm for hurt or angry feelings. Psychotherapists have worked to help their clients to forgive, and some have written about the importance of forgiveness. Until recently, however, the scientific literature has not had much to say about the effect of forgiveness. But that's starting to change. While the scientific study of forgiveness is just beginning—the relevant intervention research having been conducted only during the past ten years—when taken together, the work so far demonstrates the power of forgiveness to heal emotional wounds and hints that forgiveness may play a role in physical healing as well.

What is intriguing about this research is that even people who are not depressed or particularly anxious can obtain the improved emotional and psychological functioning that comes from learning to forgive. This suggests that forgiveness may enable people who are functioning adequately to feel even better. Published studies on forgiveness have shown the importance of forgiveness training on coping with a variety of psychologically painful experiences. Studies have been conducted with adolescents who felt neglected by their parents, with women who were abused as children, with elderly women who felt hurt or uncared for, with males who disagreed with their female partners' decisions to have abortions and with college students who had been hurt. These studies showed that when given forgiveness training of varying lengths and intensities, participants could become less hurt and become more able to forgive their offenders.

Receiving Forgiveness

Forgiving others is powerful, according to the above study, and it brings emotional and physical benefits to your life. It also can benefit the lives of those being forgiven. Perhaps there can now be the opportunity for healing in a once-severed relationship.

Forgiveness gives us a clear conscience and the associated peace of mind. "Forgive and be forgiven" is good advice.

Let your requests be made known to God; and the peace of God, which surpasses all understanding, will guard your hearts and minds through Christ Jesus.
Philippians 4:6–7

Get Started!

1. Confess and receive forgiveness for any sin, including unforgiveness, doubt, unbelief, fear, and anything else that might be between you and God (1 John 1:9).

2. List your requests. "Let your requests be made known to God" (Philippians 4:6).

3. Take authority over the enemy. Pray that God will "overthrow and overturn the works of darkness" (2 Chronicles 25:8).

4. Pray in detail. Make specific (scriptural) requests to the Father in Jesus' name. You can always add "If it be Your will" to the end of a prayer if you don't know the will of God.

5. Place your trust in His specific promises. Know that we rest our faith in who God is, in His integrity, and in the integrity of His Word.

6. Thank God and praise Him for what He *is doing according to His will.* "By prayer and supplication with thanksgiving, let your requests be made known to God" (Philippians 4:6).

What Is GOD'S Part?

God is faithful. His promises are true (1 Corinthians 1:20). His Word is true (Romans 3:4). He will watch over His Word to perform it (Isaiah 55:11). So, when you find promises upon which to rest your faith, God is pleased. He will hear and answer you. You must realize that God has more love and understanding for His creation than we can possibly comprehend. He is also more powerful than we can grasp.

Remember

- There is joy in knowing that God is alive and well and that He is interested in you! He wants to answer your prayers. Did you know that in two of the Gospels it says, "Everyone who asks receives" (Matthew 7:8; Luke 11:10)?

- Jesus said to ask and we would receive that our joy be full (John 16:23–24). The answer comes when you pray in line with God's Word. You will get results when you follow the scriptural principles in this chapter.

CHAPTER SEVENTEEN

God's Promises

BELONG TO YOU

You can trust in and rest your faith upon the promises of God when you pray. This book contains the promises related to your core needs. Keeping your mind on Jesus and praying about everything will bring great victory.

The Promises Are Yours

The Bible tells you that all provisions, or promises contained in His Word, belong to you. "Then Peter opened his mouth and said, 'In truth I perceive that God shows no partiality' " (Acts 10:34). The promises contained in the Bible, He gives to all Christians today.

*As His divine power has given to us all
things that pertain to life and godliness,
through the knowledge of Him who called
us by glory and virtue, by which have
been given to us exceedingly great and
precious promises, that through these you
may be partakers of the divine nature,
having escaped the corruption that is in
the world through lust.* 2 Peter 1:3-4

He Will Answer YOU!

*If you abide in Me, and My words abide
in you, you will ask what you desire, and
it shall be done for you.* John 15:7

*So shall My Word be that goes forth from
My mouth; it shall not return to Me void,
but it shall accomplish what I please, and
it shall prosper in the thing for which I
sent it.* Isaiah 55:11

*And what is the exceeding greatness of
His power toward us who believe, according to the working of His mighty power*

which He worked in Christ when He raised Him from the dead... Ephesians 1:19–20

Be anxious for nothing, but in everything by prayer and supplication, with thanksgiving, let your requests be made known to God and the peace of God, which surpasses all understanding, will guard your hearts and minds through Christ Jesus. Philippians 4:6-7

And whatever you ask in My name, that I will do, that the Father may be glorified in the Son. If you ask anything in My name, I will do it. John 14:13–14

And in that day you will ask Me nothing. Most assuredly, I say to you, whatever you ask the Father in My name He will give you. Until now you have asked nothing in My name. Ask, and you will receive, that your joy may be full. John 16:23–24

Now to Him who is able to do exceedingly abundantly above all that we ask or think, according to the power that works in us, to Him be glory in the church by Christ Jesus to all generations, forever and ever. Amen. Ephesians 3:20–21

And my God shall supply all your need according to His riches in glory by Christ Jesus. Philippians 4:19

Now this is the confidence that we have in Him, that if we ask anything according to His will, He hears us. And if we know that He hears us, whatever we ask, we know that we have the petitions that we have asked of Him. 1 John 5:14–15

Jesus' Words

Matthew 6:5–15 contains "The Lord's Prayer." Look at it! Live the adventure in prayer. Life with Christ. Walk in Him! God loves YOU.

Part Three

Prayer Journal

Today's Date_____

My Prayers...

_____

_____

_____

_____

_____

_____

_____

_____

_____

_____

_____

_____

_____

_____

_____

_____

_____

_____

_____

_____

_____

*Today's Date*_____

My Answers...

_____

_____

_____

_____

_____

_____

_____

_____

_____

_____

_____

_____

_____

_____

_____

_____

_____

_____

_____

_____

_____

_____

_____

My Thoughts...

---

*Today's Date*_____

My Prayers...

_____
_____
_____
_____
_____
_____
_____
_____
_____
_____
_____
_____
_____
_____
_____
_____
_____
_____
_____
_____
_____
_____

*Today's Date*_____

My Answers...

_____

_____

_____

_____

_____

_____

_____

_____

_____

_____

_____

_____

_____

_____

_____

_____

_____

_____

_____

_____

_____

_____

_____

My Thoughts...

---

*Today's Date*_____

My Prayers...

_____

_____

_____

_____

_____

_____

_____

_____

_____

_____

_____

_____

_____

_____

_____

_____

_____

_____

_____

*Today's Date*_____

My Answers...

_____

_____

_____

_____

_____

_____

_____

_____

_____

_____

_____

_____

_____

_____

_____

_____

_____

_____

_____

_____

_____

_____

_____

My Thoughts...

_____

_____

_____

_____

_____

_____

_____

_____

_____

_____

_____

_____

_____

_____

_____

_____

_____

_____

_____

_____

*Today's Date*_____

My Prayers...

_____

_____

_____

_____

_____

_____

_____

_____

_____

_____

_____

_____

_____

_____

_____

_____

_____

_____

_____

_____

_____

*Today's Date*_____

My Answers...

_____
_____
_____
_____
_____
_____
_____
_____
_____
_____
_____
_____
_____
_____
_____
_____
_____
_____
_____
_____
_____
_____

My Thoughts...

_____
_____
_____
_____
_____
_____
_____
_____
_____
_____
_____
_____
_____
_____
_____
_____
_____
_____
_____
_____
_____

Made in the USA
Middletown, DE
21 December 2021